MW01153059

HARBI GANI

(How are you?)

MAMA, BABA AND MPENDWA

(Loved one!)

This book introduces Black children to the legacy of a great man and mathematician who has left an indelible mark on the Black community and, most importantly, Black minds. **The Great Mathematician: Dr. Shabazz** was created for two reasons: to celebrate the life and legacy of a wise and respected elder, leader, mentor, and mathematician; and to encourage Black youth to believe in their mathematical ability. Before he transitioned and became an ancestor, Dr. Abdulalim Abdullah Shabazz made important contributions to the upliftment of Black communities, the Nation of Islam, Historically Black Colleges and Universities, and mathematics spaces.

Dr. Shabazz spent his life fighting for Black people. He fought against racism and injustice in educational institutions, mathematics spaces, and Black communities to create opportunities and resources for Black people to learn mathematics at high levels.

Through his dedicated work, Dr. Shabazz proved that all Black students can excel in mathematics. He debunked the myth that Black children are lazy, unfocused and incapable of excelling in mathematics. Dr. Shabazz did not believe in using standardized or placement tests to determine Black students' ability or course placement. He also did not believe in placing Black students in remedial courses. He successfully taught the students other teachers could not—those they had given up on and written off as unable to learn mathematics. As a result, Dr. Shabazz has had a direct or indirect influence on nearly half of the mathematics and mathematics education doctoral degrees earned by Black students in the United States.

Dr. Shabazz believed in the importance of teaching Black students about the monumental contributions their ancestors have made to mathematics in Africa, America, and abroad. This knowledge helps build Black students' self-esteem and confidence in mathematics.

Dr. Shabazz believed it is Black people's responsibility to educate our own and do for ourselves. Let us honor his legacy by acknowledging our contributions and believing in our abilities. Not only can Black students do mathematics, but they can perform at high levels, excelling far beyond the expectations of others!

WE HOPE YOU ENJOY THE STORY!

Sekou stared up at the framed portrait on the wall. “Daddy, who is that man?” he asked with his finger outstretched toward the picture.

Daddy smiled. “That’s Dr. Shabazz,” he said.

“Dr. Shabazz? Who is that?” Sekou asked. He
to be someone important if Daddy
wall.

Daddy took a moment to wipe the dust from the glass frame. “Dr. Shabazz was my mentor. He was my mathematics professor at Lincoln University.”

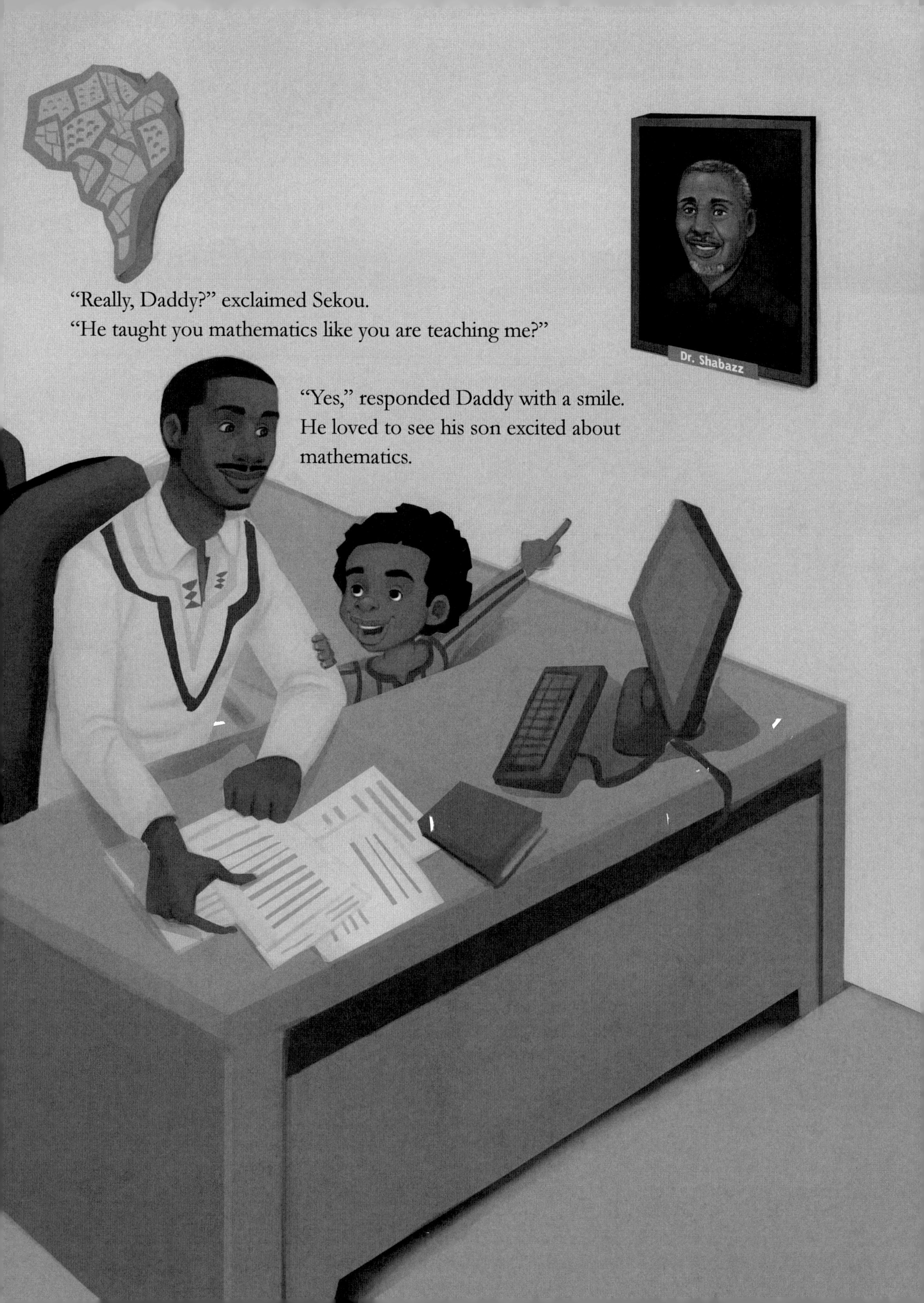

"Really, Daddy?" exclaimed Sekou.
"He taught you mathematics like you are teaching me?"

"Yes," responded Daddy with a smile. He loved to see his son excited about mathematics.

Sekou made a curious face. "What's a mentor?" he asked.

"A mentor is someone who takes you under his wing to teach or guide you," Daddy explained.

Sekou was fascinated. He wanted to know more.

"Daddy, where did Dr. Shabazz go to college?" he asked.

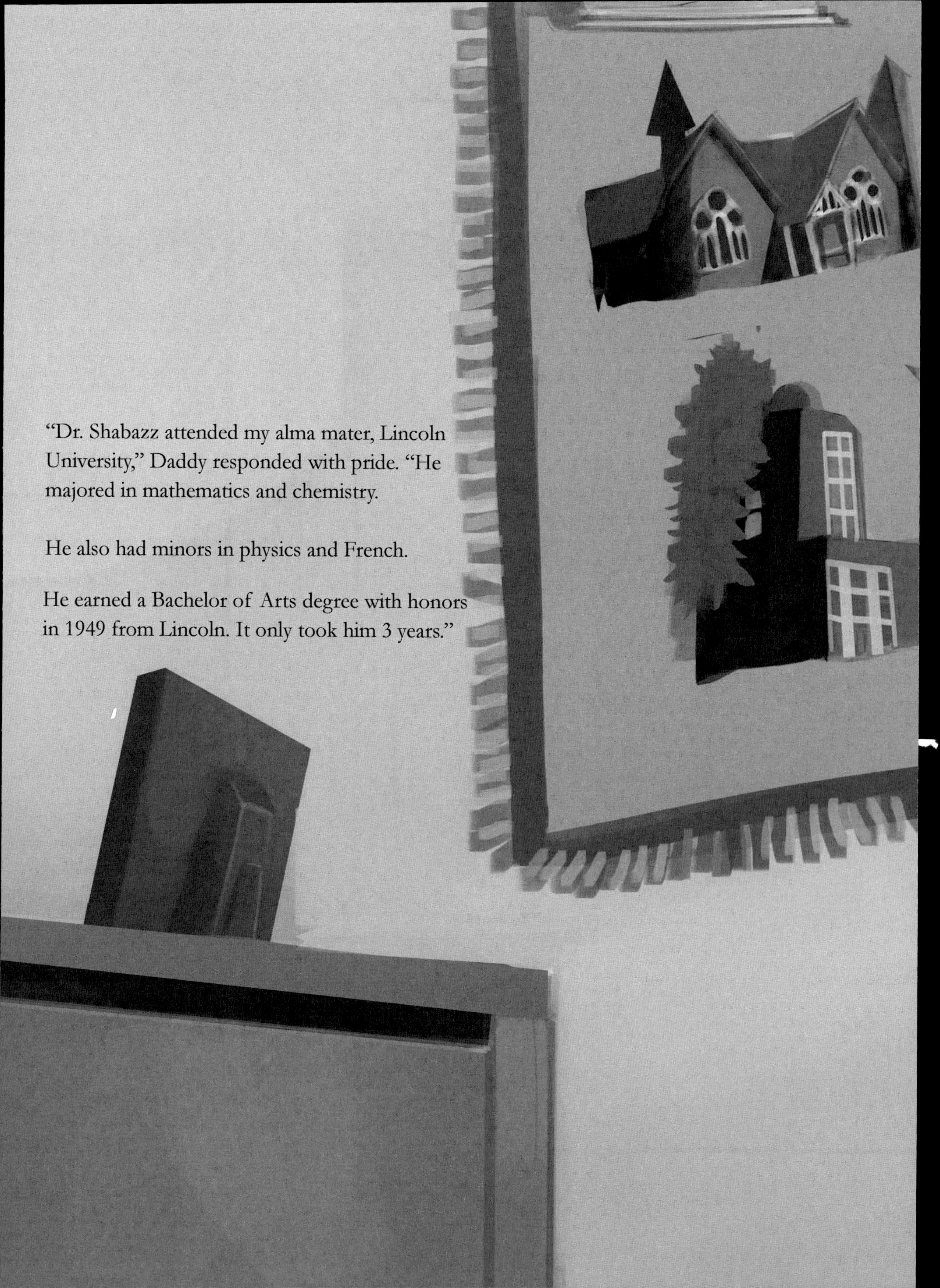

"Dr. Shabazz attended my alma mater, Lincoln University," Daddy responded with pride. "He majored in mathematics and chemistry.

He also had minors in physics and French.

He earned a Bachelor of Arts degree with honors in 1949 from Lincoln. It only took him 3 years."

"Whoa!" said Sekou. "So, Dr. Shabazz was really smart. He earned his bachelor's degree with a double major and minor in all those subject areas in only 3 years!"

"Oh, yes, Dr. Shabazz was a brilliant man who loved to learn," said Daddy. "I want you to love learning too, Sekou."

"I do love learning, Daddy," said Sekou.

"I know," Daddy said. "I love that about you."

Dr. Shabazz
CELEBRATING
LINCOLN
150 • YEARS
1854 - 2004

"But that's not all, Sekou!" said Daddy enthusiastically. "There's more I want you to know about Dr. Shabazz's education. He earned a Master of Science degree in mathematics with a minor in philosophy at another university in 1951."

Sekou held up two fingers. "Dr. Shabazz earned a master's degree, too? Wow, he is really, really smart, Daddy!"

IShango
Bone

"He sure did, Sekou. Then, Dr. Shabazz earned his Ph.D. in mathematical analysis in 1955 and minored in geometry and algebra." Daddy explained.

"Daddy, I know what a Ph.D. is," Sekou said excitedly, trying to impress his father.

"Oh, really? What is it, Sekou?" Daddy pretended to be skeptical.

"A Doctor of Philosophy degree. It is one of the highest academic degrees you can earn," explained Sekou.

"You are correct!" said Daddy, impressed.

"After earning his Ph.D., Dr. Shabazz did many remarkable things to help educate and improve the conditions of our people. He taught at four different HBCUs – Tuskegee University, Clark Atlanta University, Lincoln University, and Grambling State University. At all these universities, he helped increase the number of Black people who earned a bachelor's and master's degree in mathematics," Daddy said.

"Clark Atlanta University? I remember seeing that sign when we were in Atlanta at the Liberated Minds Black Homeschool and African Centered Education Expo," Sekou recalled.

"Yes, that's right. It is in Atlanta. Sekou, did you know Dr. Shabazz helped create the *African Mathematical Genius Benne So* book we use to do mathematics? He worked with teachers at Sankofa Shule to create the book for their students," explained Daddy.

"No I didn't know that," yelled Sekou.

UGANDA
Rutanzige

FREEDOM
BLACK POWER

"At Clark, in the early 1960s, Dr. Shabazz worked with other Black people to organize demonstrations and protests. He believed in taking action against injustice," said Daddy.

"Just like Black people did in the *Delivering Justice* book we read at bedtime, Daddy," said Sekou.

"Yes, Sekou, exactly like that," answered Daddy.

"Dr. Shabazz knew Malcolm X and invited him to speak with students in the mathematics club at his university," explained Daddy.

"Wow, Dr. Shabazz knew Malcolm X? We celebrate his birthday and teachings at my school." Sekou was excited to hear more about someone he had studied in class.

"He sure did!" exclaimed Daddy. "They both were members and spiritual leaders in the Nation of Islam. Dr. Shabazz helped develop the Nation of Islam's schools for their children and helped Black children achieve at high levels academically."

Dr. Shabazz sounded like such an interesting person. Sekou could not get enough. "Tell me more about Dr. Shabazz!" he shouted.

BLACK
EDUCATION
EDUCATION FOR LIBERATION
EDUCATION FOR MY PEOPLE!!!
1900
1939
COLORED
WHITE

Daddy chuckled at his son's enthusiasm. "Well, Dr. Shabazz was involved in the Civil Rights and Black Liberation Movements. He was accused of causing student protests and unrest on Clark Atlanta's campus and in the surrounding community. After being persecuted, he left the university. But by the time he left, the number of Black students with a degree in mathematics had increased exponentially."

Sekou thought for a moment. "Daddy, I know exponentially means to get big really fast, but what does persecuted mean?" he asked with an inquisitive look on his face.

"It means that Dr. Shabazz was mistreated for standing up against injustice," answered Daddy with a serious look on his face.

"Oh, thank you for explaining that, Daddy," replied Sekou. He was not sure why someone would be mistreated for doing the right thing, but he was happy he learned a new word.

Daddy told Sekou more about Dr. Shabazz's career as a mathematics professor.

"He taught at Lincoln University as a distinguished professor and chairman of mathematics. He wanted to give back to his alma mater. He left Lincoln after being persecuted by the administration for years. His last teaching position was at Grambling State University, where he served as the endowed chair of mathematics," said Daddy. "Sekou, these are all highly respected and important positions Dr. Shabazz held because of his contributions to our people. He was always looking for ways to give back," explained Daddy.

"Wow, I want to earn respected and important positions like Dr. Shabazz when I grow up," Sekou stated excitedly.

"Remember, Sekou, the most important thing is to give back to your people and community, like Dr. Shabazz did." explained Daddy. "Positions are nice, but helping our people is more important."

Dr. Euphemia L. Haynes
Grace Alele Williams
Imhotep

Daddy explained further.
"Dr. Shabazz strongly believed that all Black people could learn mathematics. He spent his entire career fighting against the belief that Black people could not or should not apply themselves mathematically, and that only white people made important contributions to mathematics."

"Dr. Shabazz was the first person to tell me about the contributions of Black people in America, Africa and abroad to mathematics," explained Daddy.

"So, Dr. Shabazz taught you everything you know and now you're teaching me?" asked Sekou.

Daddy chuckled. "Not quite everything, but, yes, he taught me a lot about mathematics and now I'm teaching you. Prior to Dr. Shabazz, I had no knowledge of Black people's contribution to mathematics. He believed knowledge of self was important in helping Black people learn. Dr. Shabazz also believed knowledge of self was important to challenging the belief that Black people were incapable of learning mathematics."

"I'm glad you taught me the importance of loving myself and mathematics!" exclaimed Sekou.

"Dr. Shabazz's legacy is proof that Black people are more than capable of learning mathematics. Through his teachings and the teachings of his students, he is responsible for over half of the Black people with a doctorate in mathematics," explained Daddy.

Sekou shouted, "Dr. Shabazz has a strong legacy and many, many students!"

"Yes, he does. He even helped me earn a doctorate in mathematics education," responded Daddy.

"I'm glad Dr. Shabazz was your mathematics professor and mentor, Daddy" said Sekou with pride.

"Me too!" Daddy said. "As you can see, Sekou, Dr. Shabazz believed strongly in giving back to his community."

"I'm going to give back to our community, too, just like Dr. Shabazz," proclaimed Sekou.

Daddy smiled.

THE
MAROON
WITH
US

“Early in my academic career, Dr. Shabazz inspired me to study mathematics education and to use my knowledge to help our people and improve our community,” recalled Daddy.

“I’m inspired by Dr. Shabazz, too, Daddy,” said Sekou.

Daddy put his arm around Sekou’s shoulder. “Sekou, you know Mommy and Daddy are raising you with knowledge of self, so you can make a contribution to the upliftment of our people and communities.”

“Yes, Daddy, I know. I’m going to make you and Mommy, our people, our community, our family, and our ancestors proud,” yelled Sekou.

Malcolm X
Martin Luther King Jr
rvey

“Sekou, Dr. Shabazz is no longer with us. He has transitioned from being a wise elder to an ancestor,” explained Daddy.

“I was wondering why you said his name during libations, Daddy. He has lived a life worthy of being called an ancestor,” Sekou said happily.

“Dr. Shabazz’s picture is in my office to honor him, his impact on my life, and his contributions to our people.” revealed Daddy.

“Can you put his picture in my room, next to Malcolm X?” asked Sekou.

“Yes, Sekou, I’d be happy to put his picture on your wall. As Dr. Shabazz’s mentee, it is my responsibility to make sure other young people like you know who he is and his contribution to our people,” pledged Daddy.

"Always remember that his legacy lives on through you, me, and the other brothers and sisters who know about him and pay respect to his life's work," Daddy said.

"Yes, Daddy, I'll always remember Dr. Shabazz." Sekou said.

CULTURALLY UPLIFTING FAMILY WORK!

BLACK FAMILIES should engage regularly in culturally uplifting learning activities that strengthen and help our families learn and experience new things together. We humbly present the culturally uplifting learning activities and experiences for you to engage in by yourself, with your children, cultural children, and members of your family:

1. Self-Assessment: From childhood to adulthood, think about how you feel about your ability to do mathematics. Do you see yourself as a capable learner of mathematics? Do you have a positive perspective of mathematics? Are you knowledgeable of Black people's contribution to mathematics in Africa, America and throughout the Diaspora? Before reading this book, did you know who Dr. Abdulalim Shabazz was? Do you know any other Black mathematicians?

2. Conduct research of Dr. Abdulalim Shabazz to learn more about his childhood, schooling, career and contributions to the Black community. Read to your children books, articles, and chapters about Dr. Abdulalim Shabazz. Here are a few resources to help you:
   - Developing African Americans in Mathematics: An interview with Abdulalim Abdullah Shabazz by Gloria F. Gilmer (Sankofa World Publishers)
   - In Memoriam: Abdulalim Shabazz (Final Call)
   - Minister Louis Farrakhan's Statement on Dr. Abdulalim Shabazz (Nation of Islam)
   - Abdulalim Abdullah Shabazz (Mathematical Association of America)
   - Grace Amazing: Developing the Underrepresented in Mathematics (DrAAS. info)
   - Dr. Asa Hilliard, Do we have the "will" to educate all children? in his book The Maroon Within Us: Selected Essays on African American Community Socialization

3. Visit Mathematicians of the African Diaspora website to learn more about Dr. Abdulalim Shabazz and other Black mathematicians. Write a report about Dr. Abdulalim Shabazz and any other Black mathematician of interest to you.

4. Create positive affirmations about mathematics to post around your house or classroom.

5. Conduct research about Black people in Africa's contribution to mathematics.

ABOUT THE AUTHORS

Family Afrika is a Black family that lives in Baltimore, Maryland. They believe in the importance of Black families and children connecting, honoring and respecting our cultural heritage and traditions in Africa, America, the Caribbean, and the Diaspora. As a family, we work hard to learn about our cultural heritage and traditions. We practice the Nguzo Saba (The 7 Principles of Blackness) in our everyday lives and give back to our community.

The stories presented in our books are fictionalized accounts based on real events in our family and our journey to live a life that connects, honors, and respects our cultural heritage and traditions. Reading should be a regular occurrence in Black families, and it is important for Black children to see images that look like them in the books they read.

Becoming parents and watching our son, Sekou, grow up inspired these books and the stories in them. Sekou is a co-author because he has contributed greatly to the books. Mama and Baba use his name as co-authors of the books to honor his contributions. We use Afrika as our last name to represent our quest to positively uplift our cultural heritage and traditions originating in Africa. Sekou inspired us to live a life that more closely reflects our beliefs and political ideology. We strongly believe we have to create Black institutions to positively uplift Black families and children, and connect them to their cultural heritage and traditions.

BABA SEKOU AFRIKA, ED.D. (also known as Julius Davis) is an associate professor of mathematics education at Bowie State University. His scholarship and advocacy focuses on the intellectual and social development of Black boys and young men. He has studied and traveled to Malawi, Tanzania, and Ethiopia on the continent of Africa to learn more about our cultural heritage and traditions.

MAMA SEKOU AFRIKA (also known as Yolanda Davis) is a clinical research professional who has studied and traveled to Senegal on the continent of Africa and the Caribbean Islands to learn more about our cultural heritage and traditions.

SEKOU AFRIKA (also known as Sekou Davis) is a student at Ujamaa Shule, the oldest independent Afrikan School in the United States. He plays the Afrikan drums with his brothers and sisters at Ujamaa. To start his formal school-based academic and social development, Sekou attended Watoto Development Center in Baltimore, MD, an Afrikan-centered institution.

Asante Sana (Thank you very much) for practicing **Ujamaa** (cooperative economics) by purchasing this book and supporting our Black-owned family business.

A portion of the proceeds from this book will be used to support and sponsor efforts to culturally uplift Black children and families.

Your Support is Greatly Appreciated!

Baba Sekou Afrika, Mama Sekou Afrika, Sekou Afrika

KUJICHAGULIA PRESS

We define, speak and create for ourselves to celebrate our African and African American cultural heritage and uplift our people using our Kuumba (creativity).

Title: The Great Mathematician: Dr. Shabazz
Written by: Baba Sekou Afrika, Mama Sekou Afrika, and Sekou Afrika
Edited By: Nadirah Angail

Summary: The Great Mathematician: Dr. Shabazz was created for two reasons: to celebrate the life and legacy of a wise and respected elder, leader, mentor, and mathematician; and to encourage Black youth to believe in their mathematical ability

ISBN: 978-0-9964595-9-4

For more information or to book an event, contact Baba/Mama Sekou at books@kujichaguliapress.com.

Kujichagulia Press
P.O. Box 31766
Baltimore, MD 21207
www.kujichaguliapress.com

KujichaguliaPress

@Kujichaguliaprs

#TheGreatMathematician
#DrShabazz
#BlackChildrenLoveMathematics

51873925R00024

Made in the USA
Middletown, DE
06 July 2019